Girl in Red
and Other Poems

by **Vicki Feaver**

strangefruit

Scottish Book Trust

Contents

Marigolds

Not the flowers men give women –
delicately-scented freesias,
stiff red roses, carnations
the shades of bridesmaids' dresses,
almost sapless flowers,
drying and fading – but flowers
that wilt as soon as their stems
are cut, leaves blackening
as if blighted by the enzymes
in our breath, rotting to a slime
we have to scour from the rims
of vases; flowers that burst
from tight, explosive buds, rayed
like the sun, that lit the path
up the Thracian mountain, that we wound
into our hair, stamped on
in ecstatic dance, that remind us
we are killers, can tear the heads
off men's shoulders;
flowers we still bring
secretly and shamefully
into the house, stroking
our arms and breasts and legs
with their hot orange fringes,
the smell of arousal.

Judith

Wondering how a good woman can murder
I enter the tent of Holofernes,
holding in one hand his long oiled hair
and in the other, raised above
his sleeping, wine-flushed face,
his falchion with its unsheathed
curved blade. And I feel a rush
of tenderness, a longing
to put down my weapon, to lie
sheltered and safe in a warrior's
fumy sweat, under the emerald stars
of his purple and gold canopy,
to melt like a sweet on his tongue
to nothing. And I remember the glare
of the barley field; my husband
pushing away the sponge I pressed
to his burning head; the stubble
puncturing my feet as I ran,
flinging myself on a body
that was already cooling
and stiffening; and the nights
when I lay on the roof – my emptiness
like the emptiness of a temple
with the doors kicked in; and the mornings
when I rolled in the ash of the fire
just to be touched and dirtied
by something. And I bring my blade
down on his neck – and it's easy
like slicing through fish.
And I bring it down again,
cleaving the bone.

Beauty and the Beast

He'd eat her eventually,
when he got tired
of watching her eat:

tucking the white napkin
into the top of her blouse,
picking the flesh

off a peacock's leg
with delicate teeth,
or with her tongue

sucking a clam
from its saucer shell.
After a few nights

he couldn't face
trotting to the fields
to pounce on a sheep.

While the pearl buttons
flew off her dresses,
his belly drooped

like an empty bag,
his fangs hung loose
in shrinking gums.

He sent her home to her father;
he knew he'd die
if he didn't eat raw meat.

On the day she came back
he lay in the long grass
of the rose garden,

eyes closed, meaning
to feast on her liver.
He heard her step, tasted

something wet and salt
on his lips, sensed hands
unzipping his furry pelt.

Oi Yoi Yoi

For Roger Hilton

The lady has no shame.
Wearing not a stitch
she is lolloping across
an abstract beach
towards a notional sea.

I like the whisker of hair
under her armpit. It suggests
that she's not one of those women
who are always trying to get rid
of their smell.

You were more interested
in her swinging baroque tits
and the space between her thighs
than the expression on her face.
That you've left blank.

But her *mons veneris*
you've etched in black ink
with the exuberance of a young lad
caught short on a bellyful of beer
scrawling on a wall in the Gents.

As a woman I ought to object.
But she looks happy enough.
And which of us doesn't occasionally
want one of the old gods to come down
and chase us over the sands?

The River God

doesn't know why he's such a strong swimmer;
why he drinks nothing but frothy black Guinness;
why when he stands at the top
of a long flight of stairs
he has to struggle to stop himself
raising his arms, diving into a pool
of swaying air; why in his fantasies
the girls undress – uncovering white necks
and shoulders, brown and pink nippled breasts,
the dark nests between their legs –
among reeds, under the grey-yellow light
of willows; why the women – in bars,
airports, at the Tennis and Squash Club –
he never spends more than a night with
seem flaky, juiceless; why he wants to smear
their mouths and ears and stomachs
with slime; why the water he shakes
from his hair, that twists
off his shoulders in the shower,
glitters with sticklebacks, snails,
minnows; why his wife follows
his wet footprints with a cloth;
makes him wear slippers.

Ironing

I used to iron everything:
my iron flying over sheets and towels
like a sledge chased by wolves over snow;

the flex twisting and crinking
until the sheath frayed, exposing
wires like nerves. I stood like a horse

with a smoking hoof,
inviting anyone who dared
to lie on my silver-padded board,

to be pressed to the thinness
of dolls cut from paper.
I'd have commandeered a crane

if I could, got the welders at Jarrow
to heat me an iron the size of a tug
to flatten the house.

Then for years I ironed nothing.
I put the iron in a high cupboard.
I converted to crumpledness.

And now I iron again: shaking
dark spots of water onto wrinkled
silk, nosing into sleeves, round

buttons, breathing the sweet heated smell
hot metal draws from newly-washed
cloth, until my blouse dries

to a shining, creaseless blue,
an airy shape with room to push
my arms, breasts, lungs, heart into.

The Handless Maiden

When all the water had run from her mouth,
and I'd rubbed her arms and legs,
and chest and belly and back,
with clumps of dried moss;
and I'd put her to sleep in a nest of grass,
and spread her dripping clothes on a bush,
and held her again – her heat passing
into my breast and shoulder,
the breath I couldn't believe in
like a tickling feather on my neck,
I let myself cry. I cried for my hands
my father cut off; for the lumpy, itching scars
of my stumps; for the silver hands
my husband gave me that spun and wove
but had no feeling; and for my handless arms
that let my baby drop – unwinding
from the tight swaddling cloth
as I drank from the brimming river.
And I cried for my hands that sprouted
in the red-orange mud – the hands
that write this, grasping
her curled fists.

In Grimm's version of this story the woman's hands grow back because she's good for seven years. But in the Russian version they grow as she plunges her arms into a river to save her drowning baby.

Rope

I gripped with my feet, climbed
until I could see through the hoops
of the netball posts; slid back,
burning the skin off my fingers.
Under the mound of coarse new hair,
curved bone, secretly-folded flesh
where the rope pressed, I'd roused
a live nest: a wriggling litter
like the baby voles I'd found
in a squeaking hole in the grass –
hearts palpitating in furless,
pastry-thin sides; or featherless
chicks – all claws and beaks
and black-veined wings –
that dropped from gutters.
I had to squeeze my thighs
to stop them breaking out:
squealing and squawking
into the gym's blue steel rafters;
or scrabbling down the inside
of my legs, over whitened plimsolls,
making the games mistress shriek.

Right Hand

Ever since, in an act of reckless
middle age, I broke my wrist
learning to skate, my right hand

refuses to sleep with me.
It performs the day's tasks
stiffly, stoically; but at night

slides out from the duvet
to hollow a nest in the pillow
like an animal gone to ground

in a hole in the hedge
whose instinct says have nothing
to do with heart, lungs, legs,

the dangerous head. I dreamed of gliding
through a Breughel winter:
of sitting in smoky inns

drinking burning geneva.
My hand dreams its own dream
of escaping: a waving weed rooted

in a pool so icy and numbing
I can feel its ache
rising up my arm.

The Crack

cut right through the house:
a thick wiggly line
you could poke a finger into,
a deep gash seeping
fine black dust.

It didn't appear overnight.
For a long time
it was such a fine line
we went up and down stairs
oblivious to the stresses

that were splitting
our walls and ceilings apart.
And even when it thickened
and darkened, we went on
not seeing, or seeing

but believing the crack
would heal itself,
if dry earth was to blame
a winter of rain
would seal its edges.

You didn't tell me
that you heard at night
its faint stirrings
like something alive.
And I didn't tell you –

until the crack
had opened so wide
that if we'd moved in our sleep
to reach for each other
we'd have fallen through.

Lily Pond

Thinking of new ways to kill you
and bring you back from the dead,
I try drowning you in the lily pond –

holding your head down
until every bubble of breath
is squeezed from your lungs

and the flat leaves and spiky flowers
float over you like a wreath.
I sit on the stones until I'm numb,

until, among reflections of sky,
water-buttercups, spears of iris,
your face rises to the surface –

a face that was always puffy
and pale, so curiously unchanged.
A wind rocks the waxy flowers, curls

the edges of the leaves. Blue dragonflies
appear and vanish like ghosts.
I part the mats of yellow weed

and drag you to the bank, covering
your green algae-stained corpse
with a white sheet. Then, I lift the edge

and climb in underneath –
thumping your chest,
breathing into your mouth.

Girl in Red

I was born to a mother in mourning.

The mood in our house was black
as soft tar at the edges of pavements
I stirred with a stick.

Red was my favourite colour:
scarlet, vermilion, ruby.

At school I painted a red girl in a red wood.
'Trees are green,' the teacher said.
So I painted them green,
and she said, 'Red and green clash.'

But I wanted them to clash.
I wanted cymbals, trumpets,
all the noises of rowdy colour
to drown the silence of black.

I got my mother to make me a scarlet dress.
(I didn't care that Grandma said
it made me look like a tart).

I stole a lipstick – the sizzling vermilion
that made boys and old men look.

I squeezed into ruby high-heels
that on hot days filled with blood.

I drank tumblers of pink gin
and told my sister (sent to spy on me)
it was cherryade.

I dreamed in red: scarlet, vermilion, ruby.

And now I dream in black.

Bufo Bufo

Clown's name for the creature
in my cellar. I give him gladly

the one room I don't want –
sodden cardboard, wet dark,

the gluey varnish of slugs.
What he eats: dollops

of glassy, yellow-grey meat,
host to scavenging mites,

the only things down here
to move fast. He creeps

over the floor's uneven brick
as if movement is painful,

or crouches still, under the drip
from a leaking pipe, moist

and glistening, pumping
himself to bursting.

It's spring, when toads smell their way
to water, and the females' spawn

is strung in necklaces of black-eyed beads.
But he's my prisoner – soft, warty stone

who at night swells
to the size of a man.

Glow-worm

Talking about the chemical changes
that make a body in love shine,
or even, for months, immune to illness,
you pick a grub from the lawn
and let it lie on your palm – glowing
like the emerald-burning butt
of a cigarette.
                  (We still haven't touched,
only lain side by side
the half stories of our half lives).

You call them lightning bugs
from the way the males gather in clouds
and simultaneously flash.
This is the female, fat from a diet
of liquefied snails, at the stage in her cycle
when she hardly eats; when all her energy's
directed to drawing water and oxygen
to a layer of luciferin.
Wingless, wordless,
in a flagrant and luminous bid
to resist the pull to death, she lifts
her shining green abdomen
to signal *yes yes yes.*

Horned Poppy

Frailest of flowers, armoured to survive
at the edge of the sea: leaves
tough as holly, hugging the stem
like spiked cuffs; the bud protected
by a prickly sheath; the petals furled
like yellow parachute silk, opening to expose,
at its radiant heart, the threads
of stamens, pollen's loose dust.
It blooms at the most for an hour;
torn apart by the elements it loved.
And then the pistil grows:
a live bootlace, a fuse
of multiplying cells – reaching out
to feel between the shingle's
sharp-edged flints for a moist bed
to lay its seed; or in my kitchen,
drying in the heat, a long thin hand
summoning a salt gale, a tide to roll in
over the flat land, roaring
through the open door.

The Man Who Ate Stones

He had never felt so light:
his skin like the paper of kites,

his bones like the inside of Maltesers.
He thought he was going to float

through the roof of the house,
drifting through space

like an astronaut
untethered from his craft.

He begged his wife to hold him down
but she just laughed.

He drove to the beach, and knelt
at the edge of the sea,

swallowing pebbles to weight
his stomach with ballast.

The water was black, except where the moon
lit fires in the breaking waves.

He saw the god whose home
is under the ocean's storms –

the bubbles of his breath
shooting to the surface.

Here was another man
who had to eat stones.

He plunged into the burning water
to meet him.

Bats

Only at night, the noisy nursery wakes:
the mothers who've taken over the space
in the roof returning from insect-gathering
flights. I can hear the flutter
as they squeeze in under the eaves,
the twittering, chirruping, squeaking,
of milk-sucking, carnivorous throats.
In the day, you wouldn't know they were there,
except for a smell, made up of bits of smells
I thought I'd forgotten – a hamster cage,
grandma's fusty feather mattress,
the iron reek of a birth room.
I ought to award them honour.
I could take a broom and sweep
their hanging bodies from the beams.
Once, one flew into our bedroom, spinning
above our heads, wings like the contraptions
Leonardo strapped to the backs of men
pattering against ceiling and walls,
stirring nightmares of claws
in the hair, teeth in the neck.
It settled on top of the wardrobe.
I climbed up, saw, in the half dark,
pointed ears move. It was a baby,
just learnt to fly. I wanted it
to be mine: to feed it like my daughter
feeds my granddaughter on the choicest
delicacies, to go out into the wet fields
and search for beetles and crane flies
and moths, to make it a doll's
soft cot, to rear it with the man
who pulled a sock over his hand
and gently lifted it up, launching it
through the window, returning to the bed
where care is not for the flesh of our flesh
but flesh itself, hands, tongues, the body's
tenderest morsels, offered from each
to each, shared like food.

The Gun

Bringing a gun into a house
changes it.

You lay it on the kitchen table,
stretched out like something dead
itself: the grainy polished wood stock
jutting over the edge,
the long metal barrel
casting a grey shadow
on the green-checked cloth.

At first it's just practice:
perforating tins
dangling on orange string
from trees in the garden.
Then a rabbit shot
clean through the head.

Soon the fridge fills with creatures
that have run and flown.
Your hands reek of gun oil
and entrails. You trample
fur and feathers. There's a spring
in your step; your eyes gleam
like when sex was fresh.

Killing brings a house alive.

I join in the cooking: jointing
and slicing, stirring and tasting –
excited as if the King of Death
had arrived to feast, stalking
out of winter woods,
his black mouth
sprouting golden crocuses.

Acknowledgements

Independent, MsLexia, New Yorker, New Writing 12 (Vintage),
Penguin Modern Poets 2 (Penguin), *Poetry Review*

'Judith' won the Forward Prize for The Best Single Poem. 'Bats' won 2nd Prize
in the National Poetry Competition.

With grateful thanks to Robin Robertson at Jonathan Cape.

Vicki Feaver's new collection *The Book of Blood* will be available
from Jonathan Cape in 2005.

Scottish **Book** Trust

Sandeman House
Trunk's Close
55 High Street
Edinburgh EH1 1SR
0131 524 0160
www.scottishbooktrust.com

ISBN: 1 901077 16 0

Scottish
Arts Council

Published with the support of the Scottish Arts Council Writer's Factory

A *strangefruit* production from Scottish Book Trust
for National Poetry Day 2003
"Appetite grows by eating" (Rabelais)

Vicki Feaver is the author of two collections of poetry: *Close Relatives* (Secker, 1981) and *The Handless Maiden* (Cape, 1994) which was given a Heinemann Award and shortlisted for the Forward Prize. A third collection, The Book of Blood, is to be published by Cape in 2005. A selection of her poems is also included in *Penguin Modern Poets 2*. Widely anthologised and critically acclaimed, her prize-winning work has secured her a Hawthornden Fellowship, an Arts Council Grant, and a Cholmondeley Award for distinction as a poet.

Born in Nottingham in 1943, Vicki Feaver took degrees at Durham and London Universities, lived in Brixton in Inner London for twenty years where she brought up four children, and ended a teaching career as Professor of Poetry at University College Chichester. Two years ago she moved to the village of Dunsyre at the edge of the Pentlands. This is significant, both for the wildness of the place – nature is a frequent theme in her work – and for its proximity to the homes of two of Scotland's major male poets: Brownsbank, Hugh MacDiarmid's former cottage, and Stonypath, Ian Hamilton Finlay's poetry garden. She is not out of place. With its distinct woman's voice and preoccupation with fairy-tale and myth her work presents an equally subversive vision.